IMAGES
of America

NEWMARKET

IMAGES
of America

NEWMARKET

Christopher W. Hislop

ARCADIA
PUBLISHING

Published by Arcadia Publishing
Charleston, South Carolina

Library of Congress Control Number: 2013943213

For all general information, please contact Arcadia Publishing:
Telephone 843-853-2070
Fax 843-853-0044
E-mail sales@arcadiapublishing.com
For customer service and orders:
Toll-Free 1-888-313-2665

Visit us on the Internet at www.arcadiapublishing.com

Dedicated to Ann and Robert Boulanger (Nana and Pépère). Your undying love and effortless inspiration are forever a part of my everyday existence.

CONTENTS

ACKNOWLEDGMENTS

I would like to thank John Carmichael, David LeGault, and Michael Provost for the endless amount of service they provide for this town and that was kindly afforded to me in my quest to make this book a reality. Their wisdom and loyalty pertaining to the town of Newmarket is beneficial and limitless. I have a feeling their contributions do not go unnoticed, but if they do, here is the shout-out. Thank you, fellas.

To my wife, Leigh, who has shared many of life's grand ups and downs while residing in Newmarket with me for over a decade: thanks for sticking with me, and for gifting me the two greatest things I have ever known—love, and our son, William James, who inspires me infinitely with every new step he takes and every fresh smile he flashes.

I would also like to thank Redford, Chloe, and Sassy, who have all in their own unique ways taught me that sometimes it's as simple as letting your guard down and seeing where the river intends to take you.

To the rest of my family, yes, you are all a part of this too. Without your support and shared wisdom, I wouldn't be the person I am today. Thank you.

All images appear courtesy of the Newmarket Historical Society.

INTRODUCTION

Newmarket, New Hampshire—legendary folk singer and former resident Bill Morrissey pays homage to the quaint town in his song "Small Town on the River," in which he observes, "It's just a small town on the river, nothing but a small town on the river." But Morrissey knew that there was much more to it than that. Within the confines of the four-minute tune, he sings of the mills—of the industry that thrived and continued on for over a century, very much defining the town. He references the Lamprey River (presumably named after the lamprey eels which run rampart in the waters), a river that is as defining of the mills as the mills were of the town. He sings of war and of Newmarket's loyalty to the United States in sending many of the town's residents to fight in conflicts from the French and Indian War, the Civil War, both world wars, on up through present day. Newmarket has a rich military history as well, which is celebrated in the heart of the downtown in the form of the great bandstand that pays respects to the towns many war veterans. Morrissey sings of hard work, hard times, life, community, and characters that reside in said community—good and bad. Yes, the chorus of Morrissey's song rings true; Newmarket is a small town. However, as the town's history suggests, big things can exist within a small package.

Newmarket (spelled "New Market" in the early days and morphing into a single word sometime after South Newmarket split from the town and became Newfields in 1849) was incorporated on December 15, 1727. The incorporation status came after citizens successfully petitioned the Colonial government in Portsmouth to establish themselves as a their own parish so they would not have to pay taxes to Exeter. Incorporated in 1727, Newmarket was settled far earlier than that.

Native Americans resided in what is known to us as the Lamprey River Village. They were the Squamscotts—part of the Pennacook group of Algonquian speakers. They fished using nets, self-carved hooks, and weirs, which are essentially structures built in bodies of water out of timber and netting (they are still set up and used in the Lamprey River today), harvested the oyster beds around the area, and farmed. The tribe lived in wigwams on the banks of or around the Piscassic River, the largest branch of the Lamprey. It is noted that the Native American name for the river was Pascassooke, which means "Great Pine Place."

And then came settlers from England. Newmarket was a place where early English settlers could hang their coats and establish their own ways of living from commercial and religious standpoints.

Edward Hilton (along with others, presumably) sailed from London and up through the currents of the Piscataqua River in 1623 to become noted as the first English settler in New Hampshire. The land he made home is now known as Hilton's Point (Dover), and descendants of Hilton still reside on Newmarket soil today due to land he was granted by King Charles I in 1631. The document is known as the Hilton Patent (or Grant).

Around the same time, David Thompson arrived with a fleet of Englishmen and women and settled at Odiorne Point in Portsmouth (now a part of Rye). Thompson technically arrived in New Hampshire before Hilton, but he did not stay, thus making Hilton the first official New

Hampshire resident. Nonetheless, both men and their respective crews were the first to tap into the fertile grounds of the Lamprey Village.

The natural abundance of the great salt marshes, which could be harvested and fed to livestock; the Indian weirs, which allowed for a healthy harvest of fish year-round; the lush soil around the Lamprey Village that made farming plentiful; and the virgin forest that was ready-made for the new burgeoning timber and shipbuilding industries were all reasons for the new settlers to set anchor and stay along the banks of the Lamprey. The expanse of salt marshes allowed them to harvest the hay, which could keep the livestock through winter months until pastureland could be cleared. The weirs provided runs of fish, which could be dried or salted and preserved for food. In addition to seeking a new home, English settlers were here for commerce and accompanying financial gain, which is part of the origin of the town officially becoming known as New Market. The Squamscotts migrated to an area on the Hudson River near Troy, New York, in 1672.

The earliest incarnation of mill buildings and subsequent milling industry popped up in 1640 at Squamscot Falls. It was a gristmill to grind grain. From there, sawmills were introduced to the region beginning in 1647 to ease settler concerns in producing proper shelter. The sawmills were constructed to process lumber for use in building homes, which eventually led to the production of stave pipes, hogshead or barrel staves, fencing materials, boards and joists, and bolts and masts. In short, the shipping industry started to take shape in and around Newmarket. Sawed lumber was exported predominantly to the West Indies via the Lamprey River. In exchange, locals imported such goods as molasses, rum, and sperm oil.

Further mill advancement showed up in the way of a two-story fulling mill that stood on the west bank of the Lamprey. The fulling mill afforded farmers the opportunity to bring raw wool rolls they produced up to the second story to have the wool carded. The lower story was used to full the wool, cleaning and thickening the woven cloth, and then dyeing it if color was desired. This early fulling mill was a precursor to the industrial-grade mills that would line the banks of the Lamprey River over a decade and a half later and turn Newmarket into the historic mill town it is remembered and known as today.

In 1822, the Newmarket Manufacturing Company was incorporated, and the construction of mill "No. 1" commenced the following year, wrapping up in 1824. Newmarket now had its own cotton textile manufacturing operation, which would act as the crux of the town's economy for a touch over a century. Mill No. 1 operated a total of 2,560 spindles. In total, seven mills and the great weave shed were built in the town. Newmarket Manufacturing Company dominated the town's waterfront—harnessing waterpower at the falls to power a portion of the mill's operative workflow. The company closed up shop in 1929. In the 1970s, the mill served as the headquarters of the Timberland Company during the years when it transformed itself from a small work-boot manufacturer to a leading "urban" fashion brand.

Today, Newmarket's mill buildings have been listed in the National Register of Historic Places and adapted for modern commercial and residential uses. The vibrant revitalization of the downtown has given Newmarket the face-lift it needed to once again become a vital, economically stable, and culturally significant home to its residents and a destination stop for travelers coming from nearby or afar.

One

AROUND TOWN

In the northeast corner of Rockingham County lies Newmarket, a proud New England town that packs a lot into 14.2 square miles of total space (land and water). With its workplaces (Newmarket was once the sixth-largest manufacturing community in New Hampshire), markets, shops, eateries, entertainment establishments, and public service facilities, the tiny town on the river has a lot to offer. Back in a time, when nobody had vehicles to cruise around in, it was imperative that the citizens that took residence in Newmarket had all the necessities they would need to sustain a healthy life from physical, mental, and spiritual standpoints. The town seemingly had markets on every corner back in the 1800s and well into the 20th century. Its resurgence of late (with the recent renovations of the mill buildings) has brought it back to a similar communal aesthetic feel here in the 21st century as well.

Judging by the photographs contained in this book, it is easy to drop the clichéd phrase "the more things change, the more they stay the same." Newmarket has come a long way. Pictures of faces that leaned up against the stone and brick walls running up and down Main Street a hundred years ago are replaced by the faces of today. They tell a familiar story, that Newmarket has long been a place where everyone knows everyone else's name, where they come from, where they have been, and where they are going. Each individual's story is another's story, and vice versa.

This chapter aims to shed a little light on just what was happening in Newmarket back when it had made a name for itself as a hardworking mill town where time clocks were punched and the community was provided for.

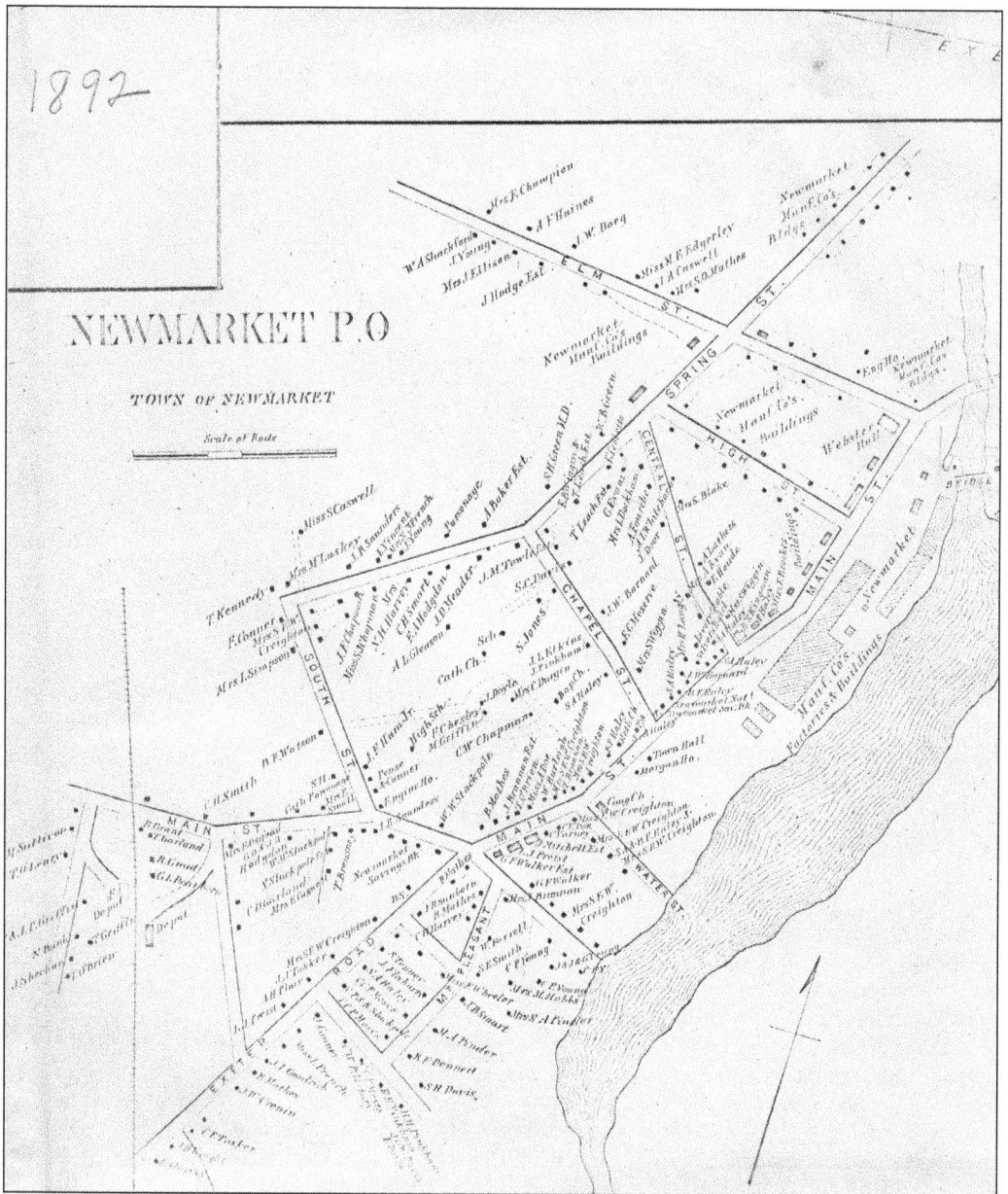

Newmarket's post office produced this now faded map in 1892. This particular section primarily depicts the downtown, which is interesting because it shows just how little space was wasted, even back then. It also shows how the town is literally built right alongside the Lamprey River. All historic locations are listed on the map, but none stick out as clearly as the mill buildings, which are visually depicted along with their names. The map speaks to the power of the mills and just how much they meant to the town. The mills are not mere dots on the map; they are spelled out and drawn. Another interesting item to note is all of the "Newmarket Manufacturing Buildings" entries, which show the housing the mills provided employees. There are many such locations throughout the downtown area, as a walk to work was in the best interest of all parties involved.

Durham Side Bridge is the main entrance to town when traveling south from the college town. Commuters see Newmarket's John Webster Library on the left, which is an architecturally unique and interesting building.

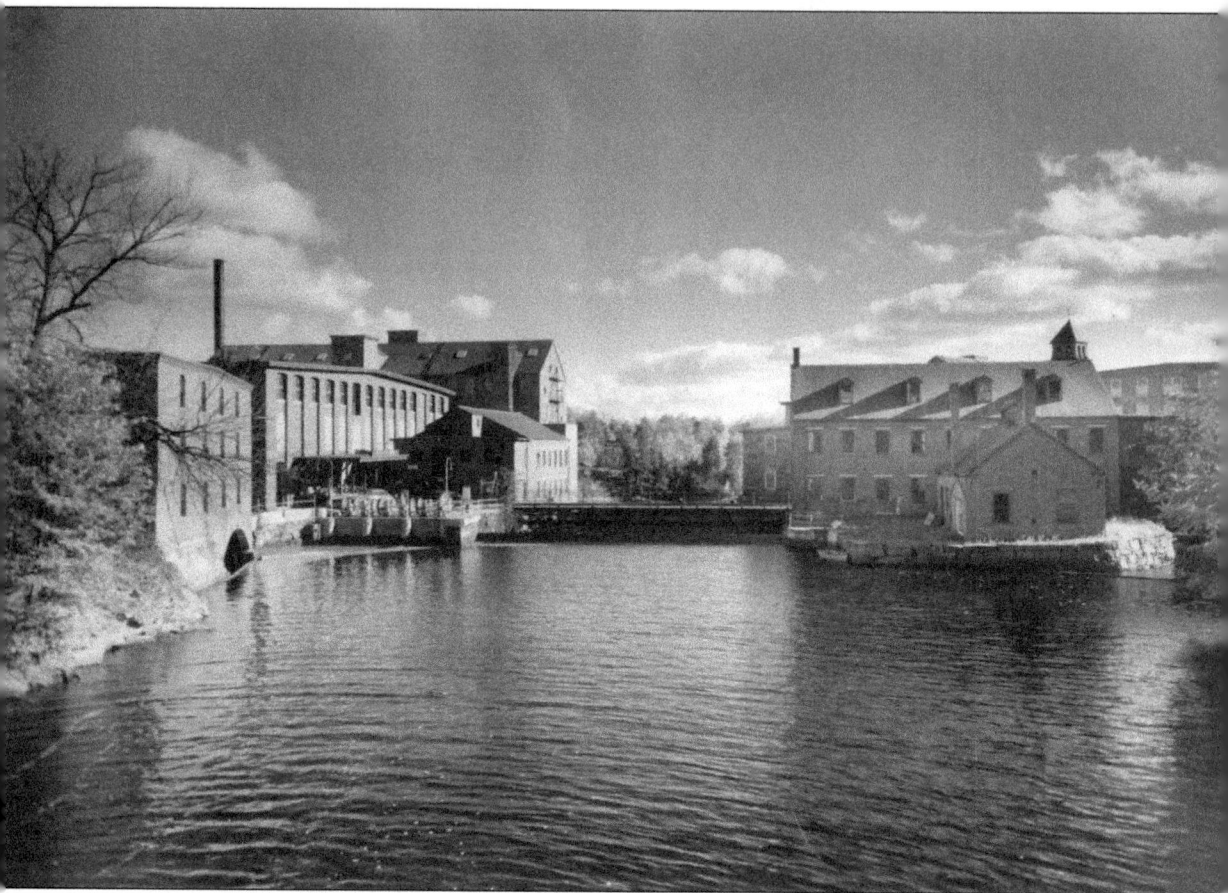

The view pictured looks downstream toward the beginning of the mill buildings, with facilities sitting on both sides of the river. To the left of the scene is Mill Building No. 3's sluiceway, a canal that sent water right to the facility, which was powered by water.

Here are two photographs of Newmarket's original town hall. The image at right offers more of a frontal view. To the left of the building are the mills. This particular mill building would later become home to the first residential units to be built out after the industrial purpose of the facilities ceased. Today, the mill is called Rivermoor Landing. The view in the photograph below gives the vantage point of looking north up Main Street The town hall is located between the old Newmarket House and the mills. The older town hall (pictured here) burned down in 1987, so the town offices relocated down Main Street to the former St. Mary's School, where they still are today. Old town hall was actually a gift to the town from the mills, providing the townspeople a place to gather and produce or host entertainment outside of an ecclesiastic setting before many of the fraternal organizations came into being in the latter 1800s.

The view in the above image is an inside look at the original town hall as it was decorated in ornate fashion for the 1899 Last of the Century Fireman's Ball. Both photographs depict the great care that was taken in hanging cloth streamers from the ceiling. The image below showcases similar decor for the Knights of Pythias May Day Ball of 1900 and demonstrates the addition of electricity to the facility within a five-month span.

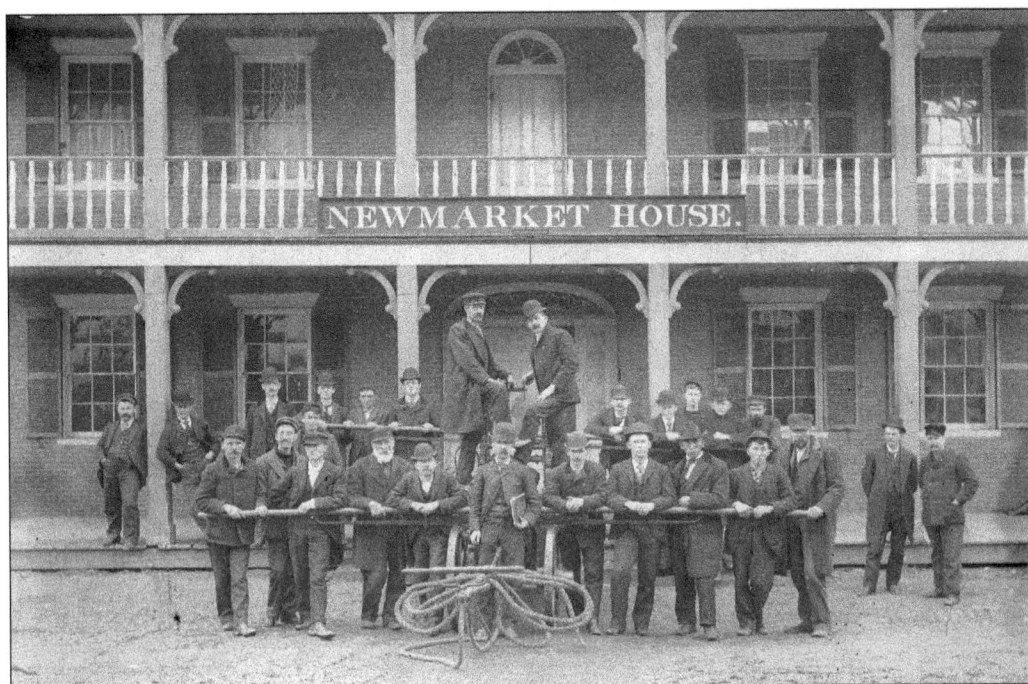

The Newmarket House (originally known as the Morgan House) was one of two well-established hotels in the downtown area. Pictured in front of the hotel in the photograph above is the Newmarket Fire Department. The hotel also boasted a sit-down dining room (the kitchen is pictured on page 22). The image below shows the common area of the hotel, where folks socialized or just hung out as seen here. Notice the moose heads on the wall. Taxidermy was very popular, and the town even had a gun club, which made hunting expeditions a regular activity that was typically followed by taxidermy if the excursion proved successful.

Hotel Willey was the second of the two well-established hotels in Newmarket. While the Newmarket House no longer exists (it burned down), the Hotel Willey still stands today, set back just a touch from the rest of the buildings in the center of downtown, directly across from the bandstand. Posing in front of the hotel in this photograph is the Fraternal Order of the Eagles (a benevolent organization). At left is Willey Court, which is where livestock were raised behind the establishment to be used as nourishment for hotel patrons. Many homes around town had similar additions attached to them for the same purpose. Residents either purchased meats from the local butcher or raised and processed their own.

The image at right shows downtown Newmarket prior to electricity. Horse-drawn carriage is the mode of transportation, and this particular rig is trotting by J.B. Silvers Hotel, the precursor to the Hotel Willey. The photograph below shows the intersection of Main Street and Tenney's Corner, which is not far from where the trio in the dual-horse carriage is in the road. Note the vast electric lines stemming from the poles at what is known as Tenney's Corner. At Tenney's Corner, one can bear right to continue on to what eventually becomes South Main Street (west of the railroad bridge) or bear left and continue on toward Stratham and Exeter.

The above photograph gives insight into how heating oil was delivered in 1905. The business was Covey's Oil Service, and this particular delivery is taking place at Lafrance's Meat and Groceries. The horses for this operation are a bit bulkier in order to handle the task with ease. The image below depicts Babe, the horse, and driver Clyde Blanchette, who are leaving the very same store after (what looks like) making a delivery of their own. For those that could afford a horse, it made transportation much easier. The horse was especially necessary for conducting business in and about town as a vendor.

Blacksmith Albert Temple Stackpole made his living producing shoes for the town's trusty steeds at his shop, located at 13 Water Street (which, in later years, was the late dining establishment Joyce's Kitchen). Tradesmen were very much in high demand during these times, and the need for horseshoes was great. As with automobile tires or the shoes on one's feet, it was imperative that the horse had a good set of treads. This downtown winter scene showcases sleighs used during the winter. Due to the cold and sometimes inclement weather, the owners of these particular horses have outfitted them with warm blankets.

M.T. Kennedy's market on Main Street was multifaceted. This was how storeowners could differentiate themselves from the competition that existed on every corner and in every alley in 1905. Not only did Kennedy sell groceries, he also had a selection of boots and shoes that were available for his customers to purchase. Kennedy also offered a delivery service, which is seen in the above photograph. The image below shows the inside of the store, where footwear can be seen, as well as applicable supplies to the left, while canned goods and crates of other groceries line the walls and floors. Kennedy leans against the counter right near the large, ornate cash register. M.T. Kennedy's building was at one time owned by historic Newmarket figure Wentworth Cheswell.

Bert Tibbetts and Varney's Market were in direct competition back in 1910. Both were butchers, and both had their regular customers. A person would often purchase his or her meat from whichever purveyor was closest to home, which would assure the freshest meat and, in most cases, a less taxing walk. Below, Tibbetts displays his meat right on the butcher block (notice the price tags sticking out). Varney is involved in a catchy marketing campaign showcasing his boiled hams, with a decked-out float for the Fourth of July parade, which was a big event in town.

The kitchen in the Newmarket House likely sourced ingredients for the fare it produced from Varney's, as they were neighboring establishments. The kitchen was an addition to the Newmarket House in the early 1900s, giving folks even more reason to visit. Not only could a visitor (or resident) get a room, but now one could have meal as well (with or without the room).

Caswell's Market was yet another grocery store in town. Caswell took great pride in displaying his products, as evidenced by the fruit neatly situated near the door for a customer to take notice of upon entering the store. Caswell's was at the current site of long-standing Newmarket dining establishment the Riverworks, located at 164 Main Street. The marketplace, as seen here, would be the tavern entrance of the restaurant.

The Durgin brothers had a long history in town. Here is one of at least a couple of shops that the family had in Newmarket in the late 1800s and early 1900s. The Durgin family owned a number of properties, including the Durgin Block apartments that are still in town today.

People's Market was to the right of Kennedy's Market on Main Street. It is directly across the street from the former Newmarket Firehouse. Today, the building is made up entirely of residential units, but back in 1910, it was another among the wide selection of markets in town. According to the signage on the building, the People's Market offered fresh seafood, which may have helped differentiate what it had to offer.

Another member of the Durgin family, Frank H. Durgin had a grocery store right in the middle of downtown Newmarket, with giant picture windows in which he would proudly display his products. His store was one of the bigger groceries—if not the biggest. Today, this spot is the Lamprey River Tavern, a well-known eating establishment, located at 110 Main Street.

Priest's Clothing was owned and operated by notable Newmarket resident A.M. Priest, who had served as the town's clerk as well as a town representative. Priest's Clothing sold fancier garments and accompanying accessories attractive to the town's more well-to-do residents. In recent years, this space is occupied by Good Juju, located at 108 Main Street, a fine arts and crafts store selling the wares of local artisans.

H.G. Reilly's Perkins Express Harness shop was another specialty trade establishment. Reilly excelled at the craft of making harnesses for his customer's needs. Of note in this image is the wooden crate to the left marked "W.H. Conner / Newfields, N.H.," for the long-standing (to this day) purveyors of the Squamscot Beverages soft drinks. H.G. Reilly's former location is now occupied by Tail Waggers Boutique, located at 147 Main Street.

H.A. Rowton & Co. Cigars and Tobacco shop made its own cigars and sold supplies so that its customers could roll their own cigarettes. The shop was a popular one in town, as there were a lot of smokers in the early 1900s. The building, which is still standing today, is Newmarket's only existing Federal-style architecture.

There were many barbershops in town—not as many as there were groceries, but quite a few nonetheless. The specifics of this barbershop are not known, but they were all very similar at the core. The barbershop was an early day coffee shop for men, many of whom would rather be shaved by a professional rather than risk a straight edge themselves. The mugs held cakes of shaving soap, and having a personal mug was more hygienic, in addition to making sure that customers returned and were loyal. Many a boy's mark of passage to manhood was the family gift of his first shaving mug and brush.

Bouras' Ice Cream Bar was established prior to World War II. This photograph was taken after the Filion bus dropped off shift workers from the nearby Navy yard. The woman standing behind the bar here is the owner, a Mrs. Bouras, while the older gentleman holding his cone up ready for consumption is Newmarket's own Judge Griffin. The customer on far right is Eva (Demers) Carmichael, the first woman to work in the blacksmith shop at the Navy yard. Note that she is wearing a World War II shop uniform. This storefront has changed hands considerably over the years. It has gone through various incarnations as a deli, but most recently, it is a technology service shop called Geek to You, located at 156 Main Street.

B.S. Kingman's was a long-standing tradition in Newmarket for many decades. It sold an assortment of products including household items, clocks, watches, and myriad sundries. Though the shop had changed hands multiple times, the locals always referred to it as Kingman's. In recent history, the establishment has been a long-lived coffee and bookstore called Crackskull's, located at 86 Main Street. Crackskull's hosts a wide range of social events on top of being a café. Above the shop is the Masonic Hall, the headquarters for Newmarket's chapter of Masons.

Church Street is a famed hill in downtown Newmarket. It was named Church Street due to the fact that, at one point, there were four churches within eyesight along the street. At the top is the historically significant Stone Church Meeting House, which is now a music venue. Across the way is Heron Point, situated on the other side of the Lamprey River. At the bottom of the hill, on the left, was Hailey's Tailoring, a shop that was known for making uniforms during Civil War times. In the 1960s, the building was demolished to make way for a parking lot for the local IGA and, later, the Newmarket Post Office.

The great Newmarket bandstand was erected as a monument for those who served in military conflicts. Given Newmarket's rich military history, the bandstand is a permanent reminder that freedom is not free. Positioned in the direct center of the downtown, the monument was once the site of many social gatherings from speeches to concerts. It was used as a podium of sorts during parades and is a visually grabbing piece of architecture in town. Originally erected in 1921 to showcase the service of those who fought in World War I, the monument today lists those who served in World War II and displays two plaques honoring all who fought during Korea and Vietnam.

In the springtime, it is not uncommon to see this section of Route 108 flood. Notice the Ford Model T on the side of the road up ahead. If it remained parked in that spot, it was likely that particular car would turn up for work at Kenniston's Garage —once the water subsided from the garage bays, of course.

The Mobil station in this photograph is right around the bend from the old Gulf station. It is on slightly higher ground and less susceptible to springtime flooding, but it does happen. When the trees are bare, it is possible to see Zion Hill and have a clear view of the town's old high school.

Garrison-type houses were erected to help ward off the threat of Indian attacks. There were a number of them throughout Newmarket. Built by Sampson Doe in 1709, Doe's Garrison, depicted in this photograph, is one of the more well-known garrison homes in Newmarket. Doe's family lived in this home until 1778. The house is no longer standing.

The John Moody Parsonage is located on Ash Swamp Road near Rockingham Junction. Built in 1730, the parsonage is documented as being the oldest existing house in Newmarket. It also served as the first meetinghouse for people practicing the Anglican Faith, or the Church of England, as Rev. John Moody was the first preacher in town.

This is a bird's-eye view of Newmarket from Heron Point. With no foliage to speak of, one can see many of the town's well-known landmarks, from the old shipbuilding ground directly across the way to the Stone Church sitting high atop the crest of Zion Hill (in the middle of the shot).

Also visible are a piece of the mill (right-hand side of the photograph) and the old Methodist church in the downtown area, which was once the tallest structure in Newmarket.

Seen directly next to the Newmarket House, the Congregational church was built in 1828. The church's timepiece in its tower is known as the "Town Clock," which is still fully functioning today. To the right is Water Street, where the town's active boat launch is.

The construction of the Methodist church in the middle of downtown Newmarket in 1871, at a cost of $25,000, was inarguably an architectural wonder. Steeplejacks are seen waving their hats and putting the finishing touches on the building's impressive tower.

The view in these images is from the same angle as the photograph on the previous page. The difference here lies only with the inclusion of electric lines at street level. The towers were considered by locals to be the jewels of Main Street. They were also the highest points in town. In 1907, the church declared bankruptcy, and its members agreed to worship across the street at the Congregational church. The image below shows the steeplejacks back on their perch, this time starting the process of tearing down the church.

Above, the view from the Methodist church steeple was breathtaking. Given the height of the steeple, the photographer was able to capture the expansive spread of the mills (before a third story was added on the branch in the middle) throughout the downtown, as well as the river behind them. Pictured below is what the Methodist church looked like without its impressive towers stretching into the sky. The building became the town's first movie theater, initially called the Scenic Temple and then the Star Theatre. Once it became the Star Theatre, which was on the second story, Turcotte's Hardware took residence on the ground level.

Here is a relic of the Star Theatre: a ticket stub to a viewing of one of the films shown there. An admission price of 22¢ seems mighty cheap when stacked up against the cost of a movie ticket today. Notice the sales tax on the stub, which is something that would not be seen today.

This is the view looking down Church Street from the top of Zion Hill. In a perfect representation of why it was called Church Street, the Baptist church is on the left, poking up from behind the Baptist church (farther left) is the steeple of the great Methodist church, and at the bottom of the hill is the tip of the Congregational church's steeple.

40

The Baptist church stood about halfway up Church Street. Construction of the church was finished in 1841. After a mill strike that occurred during the Depression, attendance at the church greatly decreased, leading to the sale of the building to the American Legion. The building was destroyed by fire on Christmas Eve 1940.

This image of a memorial Sunday at the Baptist church offers a great look into the interior of the building. Three rows of pews provided a decent amount of seating for an otherwise quaint meeting room. American flags adorn the stage, organ (left), and podium, along with an image of Abraham Lincoln.

This is another shot of the Memorial Sunday session from a different angle. Along with service, the church was utilized for public meetings, which included lectures and revival meetings. Notice the elegant yet relatively sparse design work on the ceiling and trim. The church bought the property from the Newmarket Manufacturing Company.

The Stone Church, located at 5 Granite Street, originally opened as a Universalist church back in 1833. Many of the members were directors and stockholders at Newmarket Manufacturing Company who bought the land at the top of Church Street to construct their own church on the hill. Along with the church, the Stone School was built right next door. The Stone Church now serves as a music venue/public meetinghouse.

VIEW LOOKING S. EAST FROM TOWER
OF OLD CATHOLIC CHURCH
NEWMARKET, N. H.

The steeple that once stood atop the church (it is no longer part of the building) offered stunning views of the downtown and the best vantage point at realizing the power and beauty of Church

Street as well as the Lamprey River flowing in the background.

Col. Joseph Smith built the old Kittredge House in 1729. It was constructed with locally produced brick from the brickyard at "the Creek." The house served as another garrison-style property common in Newmarket during the time. The house was a tavern in later years and was eventually torn down to make way for St. Mary Church, which was built on this exact site.

CATHOLIC CHURCH.
NEWMARKET. N.H.
-#6-   PHOTO BY THIBAULT

As mentioned, St. Mary Church was constructed in 1898 after the demolition of the old Kittredge House on South Main Street. The building next to the church served as a rectory for Father Thomas Reilly. The church remains today, though the steeple in the middle of the roof is no longer there.

Father Reilly was a very popular man in town. He came to St. Mary Church in 1886 and was instrumental in the spread of Catholicism not only in Newmarket, but in surrounding areas as well. Reilly remained in Newmarket for the next 25 years until taking a vacant role in Dover, where he preached for a few years before passing away in 1915. He was responsible for the vision and development of both the church and St. Mary School.

Though the facade of the church is slightly blurred, what is amazing about this photograph is the sheer volume of people who attended Father Reilly's funeral in 1915. The mass of people that came out to pay their respect shows just how appreciated he was as a pastor, a townsman, and as a human being.

This image depicts the two contributions that Father Reilly made to the town of Newmarket—St. Mary Church and, to the left, St. Mary School, which later served as a general elementary school for the town after 1972. In 1987, the building became Newmarket's new town hall after fire engulfed the original town hall. This location remains the town hall today.

As the cart suggests, Provost's Express (part of Interstate Express Company) was essentially the "original FedEx." Dated 1905, the cart is seen delivering packages to the Hotel Willey. The expansive organizational method of the cart is an interesting study. The proprietor of the single-horse cart was one Charles H. Provost.

This is a picturesque view of Newmarket during winter months. The horse seen here enjoys a quick drink from the watering bowl; similar watering bowls were set out around in various spots to quench the thirst of a horse at work.

The hooded cart was a status symbol during the 1800s. This particular vehicle is thought to be a doctor's buggy. This duo trots down Main Street. In the background is a section of the mills owned by Newmarket Manufacturing Company.

Jacob's Well is another watering hole enabling folks to fill buckets and bottles with crisp, fresh drinking water. The well is located on Grant Road and still exists today. It is said that people traveled far and wide to fill up at this particular well.

Known as Great Ledge, this stone hillside is nestled right next to the Newmarket Firehouse (on the left) on Main Street. To the right is a common courtyard, which remains the same today. Atop the ledge, one would be able to easily access Zion Hill, where the Stone Church, Stone School, and original Newmarket High School reside.

A Civil War memorial was constructed by Newmarket's Grand Army of the Republic at the base of Great Ledge sometime in the early 1900s. Newmarket military men who took part in the Civil War are listed on the plaque, which is attached to the rock. A fire alarm bell tower stands at the crest of the ledge.

Fires seemed to happen often in downtown Newmarket. This particular blaze occurred in 1894, sometime before the Durgins bought the property. Four men are seen at the center of the rubble, which gives some perspective on how large the area was that was burned. Behind the rubble in the near distance are the ever-present mill buildings that are the backdrop to many downtown photographs.

The original Newmarket Firehouse sat just around the bend on Main Street. Pictured here is the crew in uniform on full display in front of its horse-drawn ladder truck. Directly to the right is Great Ledge. In the top left-hand corner, the profile of the original Newmarket High School is in plain view. The fire department originated in 1832.

Tiger No.1 was the first fire engine purchased by the fire department in 1852. It was built by E.S. Leslie in Newburyport, Massachusetts. The engine cost the town $1,000—a pricey sum back then. The engine still exists today and is on display at the original firehouse, which is open to the public during special events.

A second fire station was on Elm Street. It was built by the mills and provided sole protection for the town until Tier No. 1 was purchased. The crew here is also dressed in full uniform, and firefighters are seated and standing in front of the station's bay door, where one of the crew is perched upon another horse-drawn pumping vessel. The location on Elm Street afforded the department faster response times depending on what side of town a fire happened to flare up.

The old Stone School is atop Zion Hill and accessible directly from Granite Street. The school was built in 1842 on land given to the Universalist church by the Newmarket Manufacturing Company. The building operated as a school until 1964. At this time, the Newmarket Historical Society acquired it, and it remains the owner today. In essence, the structure is still very much an educational facility. The historical society holds endless amounts of town artifacts and other pertinent historical materials spread throughout the tiny two-story building. There is even a section that remains set up like a classroom from the days when the structure was still a schoolhouse.

The above image shows a classroom in action in the old Stone School back in the early 1900s. Art graces the back wall, while it looks like music is being taught on the chalkboard to the side. All four walls of the Stone School are lined with chalkboards, which remains true to this day. In the photograph below, a class poses for a picture in 1915. The image was likely captured outside the Stone School from the top of Zion's Hill. Right in front of the children would be the Stone Church (or the Universalist church, as it was known back then).

A fair amount of people who resided in Newmarket have been of Polish descent. To this day, there is the Polish club, where it is thought the first Polish school was operated out of. This photograph depicts one of the original classes, probably sometime around 1911.

Writing on the back of this photograph suggests that this is another class from the Stone School. In the background is a working smokestack. This image was probably captured around the original Newmarket High School. Extra credit shall be granted to those who can find the only student donning a cap in this picture.

The image at right shows the original Newmarket High School. To the left of the school would have been the Stone Church, and beyond that was the Stone School. The high school was built in 1874 out of brick. The bell tower atop the school has since been removed, and the bell housed in the tower can be found at the Newmarket Historical Society. The image below showcases the current high school, which was built in South Main Street in 1924. Talks have been ongoing for quite sometime now about the construction of yet a newer high school, but for now, this one remains.

These are profile views of the original Newmarket High School overlooking downtown. The photograph above was made in approximately 1910 with the bell tower intact. The image below shows the building with no tower, and as the words scrawled on the side of the building denote, it had been converted into a day-care center. This would have been in the late 1960s or early 1970s. Today, the building has been renovated and converted into a senior housing facility. It seems that during its long history, the structure has served the full demographic spectrum—from youth, to teens, to the elderly.

Yet another Newmarket-based school was the Durham Side School, which was further north on Route 108 toward Durham and about a mile from downtown Newmarket. It was a one-room schoolhouse for elementary-age kids that was located in what is now the home of Great Bay Dental Care, located at 48 North Main Street.

Trains played a big part in expanded transportation for the residents of Newmarket. The aptly named Newmarket Depot is captured here in the winter of 1910. It was one of the main train stations (of the two) in town along the Rockingham Junction Station that offered both commercial and industrial transportation. In this particular photograph, it looks as if a load of (perhaps empty) bread boxes is on its way back to Dover.

Above is another shot of the Newmarket Depot featuring workers, from left to right, Henry Malo, Herbert Smart, a Mr. Kidder, James Crimmins, and Grover Kenniston. Below, an engine rides the rails on the bridge over the bay on New Road, which connects Newmarket and South Newmarket (which became Newfields in 1849) to Stratham and Portsmouth. Transportation by train was pretty prevalent in these times, and tracks connected many of the towns in Seacoast, New Hampshire, to cities such as Boston and New York. Trains routes stopping in Newmarket ceased in the 1960s.

These photographs are of the annual Newmarket Day extravaganza. Once a year, Newmarket Manufacturing Company would sponsor a trip on the rails for workers and their families to spend a summer day at Hampton Beach. As seen in these shots, the first Newmarket Day depicted occurred in 1910, while the second happened in 1911. The retreat allowed mill workers the opportunity to experience the train and escape the small town, if only for a day. It was an anticipated annual event and an added perk of being an employee of the Newmarket Manufacturing Company.

The second major train station in Newmarket was the Rockingham Junction Depot, which may have actually trumped Newmarket Depot. This was one of the busiest depots in the state, with a dining room and convenience shop built right into the structure. The junction welcomed most of the major railcars that were steaming through town carrying a mix of commuters and cargo.

In any mode of transportation, there are risks involved. Accidents were no stranger to the rails leading in and out of Newmarket. There are many archived newspaper articles highlighting train wrecks throughout the course of the rail history of the area. Here, an overturned train may have been operating in less than ideal weather conditions. Also in the shot, which was captured in 1905, the snow is falling as winter presses on in the area.

Two

THE MILLS

Newmarket was and is defined by the mills. For more than a century, they formed the economic, political, and industrial fabric that held the town together. The mills and the river that framed them offered the opportunity that afforded a large number of people a sustainable existence. With roots that trace back to the 1600s and extend to a varying degree until the present day, the mills have been Newmarket's lifeblood. That is a piece of history that, though morphing, will never change.

From industrial operations to residential, commercial, and entertainment facilities, the mills *are* Newmarket. Newmarket owes its very thick historical roots to that brick, stone, and wood–crafted spine. The mills are a backbone that has certainly wavered at times, and when it has, the town has shown direct effects. However, the said backbone has never actually broken, and it likely never will.

Newmarket Manufacturing Company is responsible for cultivating the town's first fire department, the Mill Fire Squad. The company purchased the first fire engine in the town in 1832. Throughout the history of the early fire department, as town records show, the Newmarket Manufacturing Company provided much financial backing and purchased a lot of the department's equipment.

Before the mills took the town by storm, Newmarket had a substantial shipbuilding industry, as well as a burgeoning import and export operation based on the waters of the Lamprey River. In this photograph is a docked gundalow, which was a regular sight in everyday Newmarket life. This gundalow is likely unloading product for use in town stores or materials used in the mills.

Prospective mill employees may have been drawn to sign on to the workforce due to Newmarket Manufacturing Company's development of employee housing, which could be seen throughout downtown Newmarket. As is evident in the photographs, these homes were often constructed with a template design and produced in quantities to be able to assure an employee—and perhaps, his family—shelter. Below is the community known as New Village, which was located at the western end of Elm Street. Construction on this string of homes began in 1903.

The initial use of the mills and the business conducted by Newmarket Manufacturing Company was that of textile production. The photograph above shows the expansive length of the mill rooms and the number of machines that existed in each mill. Boxes of spooled thread were used in the production process. The photograph below shows the spools being collected as they are emptied, ready for respooling. Again, the depth of the rooms is a marvel, and seemingly, no space goes unutilized. These photographs are marked as being taken sometime between 1903 and 1907.

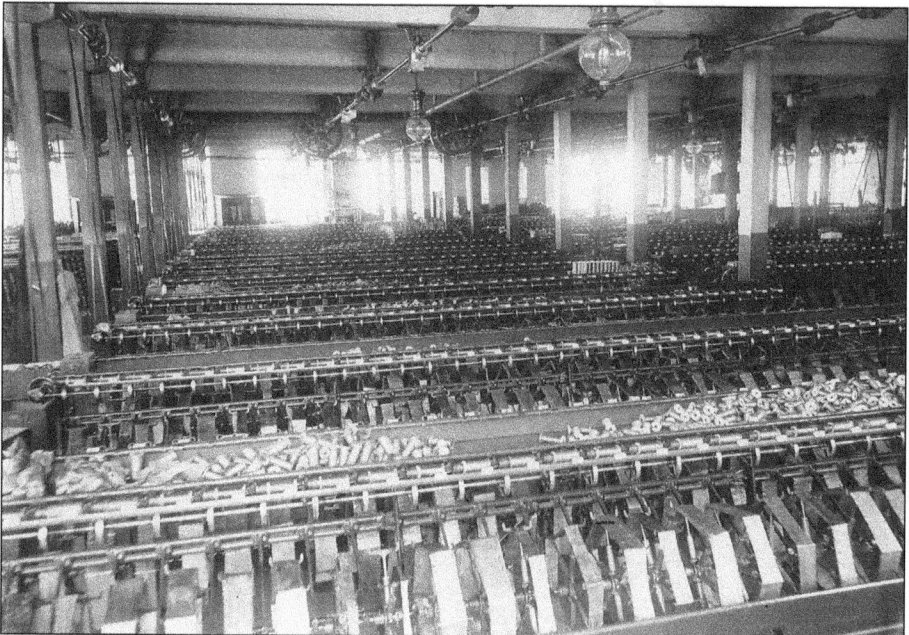

This is one of the best photographs in existence that speaks to the overall size of the rooms that workers and machines operated in. The ceilings in this particular mill building were around 18 to 20 feet high. From this vantage point, there looks to be a cleared track of sorts that allows easy navigation around the perimeter of the room, while the machines are packed in with room for some movement for operation—but not much.

There are a number of great photographs showcasing the mills from the Lamprey River. Here is a shot from 1910 that offers a good view of the town's shipyard and docking bays for recreational vessels. The other interesting element here is the thick plume of black smoke coming from the

chimney in the center of the photograph. The mills generated some energy from processing water from the Lamprey as well as burning coal.

At first glance, this photograph may appear to be that of a school's class picture. Truth be told, it is a group of mill workers getting an annual photograph taken for Newmarket Manufacturing Company's yearbook. This was a time before child labor laws, and children were employed for tasks that may have required them to fit into spaces that adults could not squeeze into.

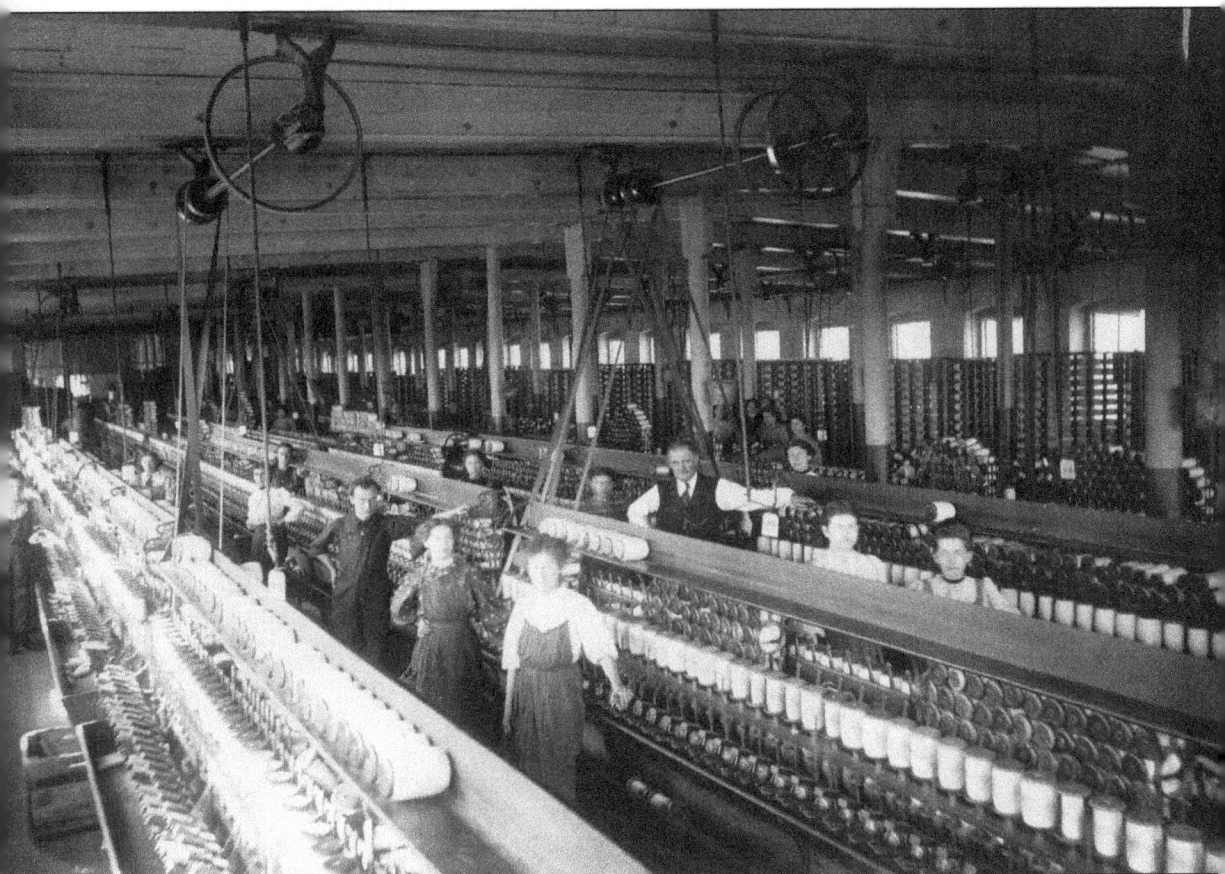

This image of the spinning room documents the span and length of the mills. In this room, empty spools were refilled or respooled with thread that could be used in the production process. It was in the best interest of female employees to pull their hair back and put it up in a contained arrangement to prevent accidents from occurring on the work floor.

Two more shots of the spinning room are shown on this page. When Mill No. 1 was built in 1824 (it was completed two years after the company's incorporation), the company had 2,560 active spindles. Mill No. 2 was completed a year later, in 1825, giving the company another 4,096 spindles to work with. Over the span of a century, Newmarket Manufacturing Company would erect seven more mills occupying most of Newmarket's waterfront and stretching across Main Street, as well as continue its dominance in acquiring real estate to expand operations in town. The company was profitable and maintained fiscal strength while bolstering the town's economy, so such expansion was generally met with little hesitation among town leaders.

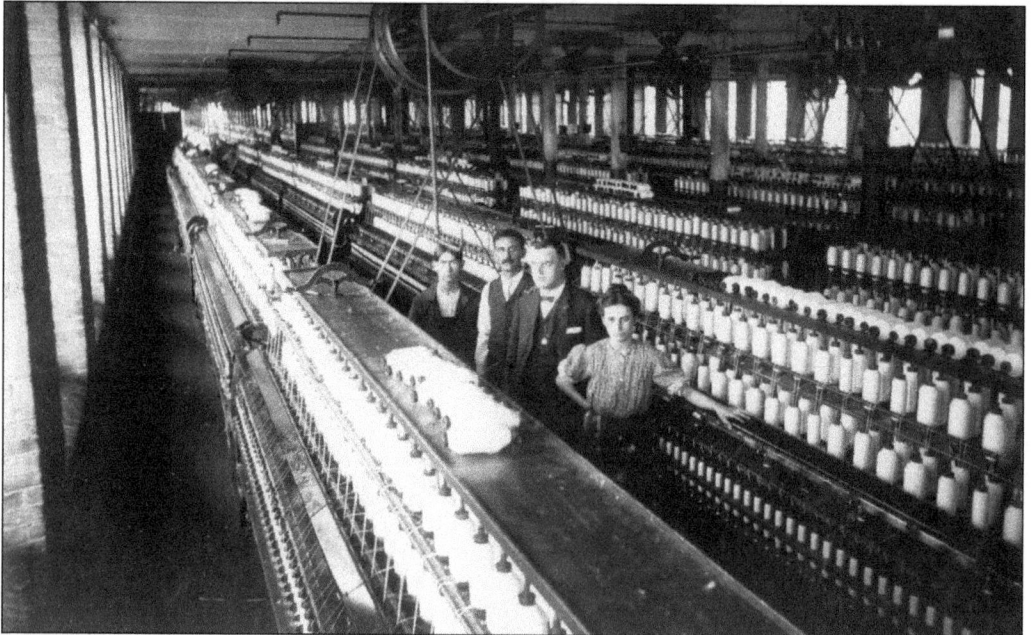

Electricity entered the picture at Newmarket Manufacturing Company in the early 1900s. These photographs show the lights that were installed, enabling work to continue into the evenings. Prior to electricity, mill work relied on the light of the sun to get production on point, hence the long spans of massive paned windows that lined every bit of the walls on either side of the mill buildings. There were also skylights, which let light in on the top floors. Once the sun went down, work was done for the day. With electricity, production shot up significantly. While the company was making more profits due to the acquisition of artificial light, employees were not earning more wages, making a maximum of $2.72 a week, thus leading to a labor dispute and walkout in February 1929.

The image above showcases the mills policy of wasting little. By hiring small children, who were know as bobbin boys or bobbin girls, the company had a piece of the workforce that could fit into tiny spaces that adults might have had a hard time navigating. Workers are making felt at the machines shown above. A part of the felt-making process would be the children sweeping up lint in and around the production machines throughout the mill operations, which was totally usable in the felt-making process. The image below is a good representation of just how many people were working in a given room and just how tight the working quarters were. This is a looming room, where kids might find lint on the floor throughout the operative process in areas where adults could not.

The upper floor of Mill No. 5 was also a haven for lint collection. Lint can be spotted flying through the air in the foreground and throughout this particular weave room. Also of note is the fact that, being an upper floor, there are skylights in place, allowing natural light in, which was highly beneficial before electricity was introduced to the mills.

NEWMARKET, MILLS,
NEWMARKET, N.H.

This is another shot of the mills as seen from the Lamprey River. Worth noting is the substantial coal pile that has amassed in the mill yard at the center of the photograph. The image also shows three working covered bridges that connected the mill buildings together.

Pictured above is the 40-ton rope drive wheel that was installed shortly after the start of Newmarket Manufacturing Company. The earliest mills that existed in region (saw, grist, fulling, and carding) at the Lamprey Falls were run exclusively by waterpower. The cotton mills were of the same operative category as those earlier mills. Later, steam was used to provide energy. A Corliss engine burned coal (seen on the previous page) to produce steam, which would power the great drive wheel installed at Mill No. 4, built in 1869, in turn operating a rope drive whose power was transferred to a leather belt that ran all the mill's machinery. The image below is that of the pumping mill, which today serves as a crucial piece of the town's water supply.

Pictured above is a boardinghouse built by the Mills to house supervisors and workers. During the construction of the mills, homes were sometimes moved to different locations to make room for mill expansion. This particular boardinghouse was no exception to that rule. When Mill No. 8, the great weave shed, was built (on the same property as the town library as seen in the photograph below) in 1917, boardinghouses such as this were moved to different locations in town to accommodate the construction. The weave shed was reportedly once the largest single room in the world, boosting Newmarket Manufacturing Company's spindle count to over 60,000.

The addition of Mill No. 8, the great weave shed, also brought with it the construction of the town's second water tower (the first was the Durham Side Water Tower). The addition of the No. 8 water tower added valuable resources to the mill facilities by way of drinking water and fire protection. Looking at the mills from the familiar vantage point of the Lamprey River, the new water tower can be spotted quickly as it stands high above the mills. It was now one of the tallest points in town as well as one of its most talked about landmarks.

Though a tad blurry, this photograph remains one of the best images of the covered bridge that spanned Main Street and connected the original mill facilities with the new weave shed. Drivers took notice of the pride exuded through the company's name that was scrawled across the bridge's outer wall.

The view for those coming across the Durham Side Bridge into downtown Newmarket included a stunning architectural achievement in the addition of the great weave shed. Emblazoned on mill No. 8's water tower is "Newmarket Mf Co. / Newmarket, NH." Of note is the glass roof of the weave shed.

A dedication ceremony was in store for the grand opening of Mill No. 8. A stage is set where mill bosses and workers would come together to chat about the prospects of the company's new addition. The view of the inside of the weave shed is quite awe-inspiring. These photographs were taken before any machinery was brought into the mill, so one can gather just how expansive the space was in this single-room facility. The addition of floor standing water bubblers is evident throughout the room.

The facility would not be complete without the addition of fire buckets. Being advocates of the Newmarket Fire Department, it only made sense that the mill would install such buckets throughout the weave shed. There also happens to be a piano on the platform in the middle of the room, adding to the festivities of the grand opening celebration.

This view from the perch of the newly established Mill No. 8 water tower is, appropriately, a shot of the original Durham Side Water Tower, just off to the left. This image also draws attention to the sawtooth design of the weave shed's roof. From the perch on the water tower, it may have been possible to spot Durham on a clear day.

Two more views from the Mill No. 8 water tower are depicted on this page. The image above offers an excellent view of the mill building and downtown Newmarket, as well as the icy waters of the Lamprey River. To the right is the original town hall, which is right next to the Congregational church. The view in the image below is slightly to the left and gives more detail of the mills across the street. This is another opportunity to see the bridge that spans from the weave shed to the mill building across Main Street.

The view in the last image made from Mill No. 8's water tower looks out toward Elm Street (on the right). Directly in the middle of the frame are residential units located on Spring Street where mill workers lived. Similar residential units are in this exact spot today. Straight down and slightly to the left is what appears to be a woman dressed in black walking along the side of the road. Her presence gives the impression of just how high this tower was.

Walter Gallant was the last standing mill agent of the Newmarket Manufacturing Company. This particular photograph, as evidenced by the calendar, was taken in 1912. When the company closed its doors for good in 1931, Gallant was the man behind the wheel. He moved all operations and equipment down to Lowell, Massachusetts.

Upon studying the history of the mills and having a look at the many historic photographs that exist in the collection at the Newmarket Historical Society, it is easy to get lost playing a *Where's Waldo?*–type game. The man seen in the two images here is named John Mills, who shows up in dozens upon dozens of local historical photographs. He was Newmarket Manufacturing Company's foreman and was thus in charge of daily operations. It makes sense then that he would pose with many of the group photographs pertaining to the mills.

Another noted Newmarket Manufacturing Company employee is loom fixer Charles Lavallee, who also shows up in a lot of local historical photographs. Lavallee was the last of the loom fixers at the mills, so everyone made an attempt at making friends with him. In order to make quota, an employee would need his machine to be running up to snuff. In order to get their machines operating efficiently and effectively, they needed Lavallee, who wore a very prominent, unique moustache, making him easy to point out in a crowd.

Newmarket Manufacturing Company took on the production of silk spinning and weaving in the early 1900s mainly because it was a better-paying industry than cotton. The con of the operation was that silk was more difficult to work with, but the company had the technology and workforce to navigate potential snags. The company manufactured silk linings for coffins, as well as more high-end pieces of cloth. In the photograph above, the looms are working to full effect. The image below depicts workers at their respective machines. Newmarket Manufacturing was a well-respected industry leader known for its efficient practice, which is evidenced in this picture by what appear to be production logs hanging in the right of this particular shot.

The image above showcases a silk preparation wheel. It is here that the silk would be unpacked and spun to fit the spools hanging and aligned behind the woman in the picture. By 1908, some 2,750,000 yards of pongees, taffetas, satins, and mulls were produced by the Newmarket Manufacturing Company annually. The image below appears to show a folding room, as evidenced by the folded textiles stacked up on the tables in the background. In total, the annual income generated from the goods produced in these mills was somewhere in the ballpark of $1.5 million.

The Newmarket Manufacturing truck replaced horse-drawn wagons when it came to transporting product in and out of the mills. Here, warehouse workers gather for a group shot before continuing with their workday. Again, as technology and practices progressed, so too did the bottom line of the company.

The aforementioned Durham Side Water Tower was the original tower that housed Newmarket's supply of water for the town before the construction of Mill No. 8's tower. The photograph depicts the noted landmark toward the end of its life. It was dismantled shortly after this photograph was taken.

Newmarket Manufacturing Company packed up and shuttled the operation down to Lowell after more than a century in Newmarket. The great weave shed was torn down after only about a dozen years in service. The foundation can still be seen, and the acreage of property that the building took up is now a municipal parking lot, as well as a reserved lot for the newly renovated mills of the present day. After Newmarket Manufacturing left, the vacant properties went through a myriad of host companies, including the Macallen Company, which switched the operative mill culture landscape in Newmarket from textile manufacturing to compressed sheet mica products; the hot-mold room pictured at right shows the new equipment.

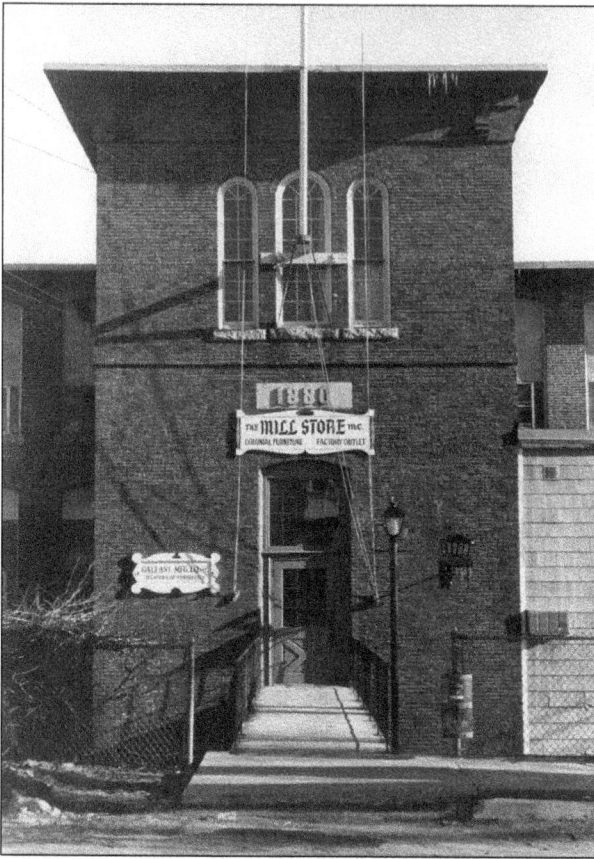

A couple of stabs at revitalizing the mill industry in Newmarket came in the form of furniture and even shoe manufacturers. The photograph at left showcases a 1970s-era Mill Store establishment that sold furniture produced in the mill building. Where the weave shed once stood was the construction of Rockingham shoe manufacturing in the late 1950s, which also eventually came down. Timberland had a successful run in Newmarket when it looked to expand the company in the mills during the 1970s before moving its headquarters to Stratham, New Hampshire. In recent years, Chinburg Builders has won several awards for its renovation of the mill building and converting it into inspired residential and commercial units that remain true to the mill's aesthetic roots with a subtle modern makeover. Downtown Newmarket has been revitalized due to the scope of this worthwhile project.

No matter what season graces Newmarket, the view of the mills from the river always looks tremendous. Here is a shot taken from an iced-over Lamprey River before the water tower was deconstructed. Also of note is that one of the three covered bridges depicted earlier is no longer in service in this photograph.

This photograph from 1887 shows the washout that occurred near the lower falls after the frozen Lamprey River thawed in the spring. Historically, this washout has happened on more than one occasion. Granted, during some years, it is less dramatic than others (a bridge has been washed out here), but residents have become wary and take precautionary measures to assure minimal damage to their property as best they can.

Three

SOCIAL COMMUNITY

Newmarket has long embraced the tradition of community and bringing its citizens and visitors together in unison. From fraternal organizations of yore to contemporary art exhibits in the renovated mill building, dancing at the Rockingham Ballroom, and steady movement high atop Zion Hill at the historic Stone Church, social activity has long been abuzz in the small town by the river.

Be it by plane, train, automobile, or horse, travel to Newmarket brings one to a culturally significant seacoast town with a unique feel that is matched by few others. From the early 1900s, city people came here seeking solitude and relaxation along the banks of the river and the bay. Indeed, many of the large old inland farms and homes along the shores of the bay welcomed summer guests and boarders. The Adams family house at Adams Point was one of the earliest in the area to set a tradition of hospitality, welcoming guests at the Newmarket Depot and then transporting them by gundalow or carriage down Lubberland (Bay) Road. Some rather famous people took the air in Newmarket at times, such as Helen Keller and Emma Borden. The practice of summer guests added much appreciated monetary gain to many farmers in the late 1800s. The practice of securing summer homes became very popular in the 1870s, as wealthy and upper middle class families looked to escape the heat and smells of summer in a large city. Many farms added enclaves of summer cottages to rent out, and some nearby places became quite popular, such as the Shirley Cottages on Packers Falls Road and Highland House on Bennet Road. Newmarket is a town where people are friendly and inviting but also know when to observe a moment of silence and bask in the togetherness of meditative relaxation. There is serenity in Newmarket that is felt by all who have experienced its beauty.

In this chapter, the spotlight turns to the characters and societal organizations that have long been permanently sewn into the cultural fabric of a town that no industrial mill is fully prepared to reproduce. The fabric of social community is in the naturally existing element of human interaction. Community cannot be found on a shelf and purchased. Community cannot be fabricated on a machine. It exists in a group of smiling faces and kindhearted souls. This, according to the evidence in the ensuing chapter, can be located in Newmarket.

Nearly everything that occurs in Newmarket begins and ends on the Lamprey River. The image above contains a collection of boats—recreational or otherwise—used for navigating the river that is so fundamental to accessing Newmarket. Fishing is a prominent hobby and was once a serious industry in town. The photograph below was made from a vessel cruising the Lamprey River's waters. The town of Newmarket is on great display from this vantage point. The waters of the Lamprey are capable of providing a great degree of energy for the mills as well as acting as an extremely calming presence.

The mouth of the Lamprey River as it winds its way from Great Bay up behind the mills was much wider in the early 20th century than it is today. This photograph, taken in 1905, is proof. The tide seems like it still has plenty of room to come in, and yet there is a very wide inlet here.

Depicted here is the immensely wide inlet provided for easier navigation of large ships such as the expansive *W.M. Davenport*, which docked behind the mills in 1906. This is a vintage photograph that hangs in the mill buildings and is the direct reason this book is being written. To imagine a ship of this magnitude sailing behind the Newmarket mills is utterly fascinating.

JULY 4TH 1910.
NEWMARKET. N.H.
PHOTO BY THIBAULT.
#73

Parades are still common in Newmarket today, but they are never quite as extravagant and as much of a production as the Independence Day celebration looks in 1910. Every business in town seems to have a float that is decked out in the spirit of the gathering. The streets are lined on both sides with onlookers. The image below showcases individual departments from the Newmarket Manufacturing Company that joined in on the celebration by crafting their own unique floats. The first float in line is the cotton department, which is followed up by the mill's baseball team.

JULY 4TH 1910.
NEWMARKET, N.H.
PHOTO BY THIBAULT.
#70
COTTON DEPT.

Newmarket's first airship is on display in the same Independence Day parade mentioned on the previous page. In a very interesting display of innovation, a young boy put this ship together and adorned it with festive decor. There was also a marketing effort in play here, which suggests that the Dearborn's Country Store may have sponsored him.

This last frame from the parade captures the Joliet Club in uniform marching in unison. The Joliet Club, or the Catholic Order of Foresters, formed in Newmarket in 1897, filling the need of impoverished immigrants who streamed into the United States seeking a better life. The group bought and operated out of the Stone Church, which it renamed Forester's Hall, from 1916 to 1948. The club is no longer active.

The Grange Fair that took place on September 19, 1907, was a marvel in its own right due to the hot air balloon rides. The fair was an annual event set up by the Grange of New Hampshire, which was formed on December 4, 1867. It was originally founded on the teachings of agriculture and was the first organization to give women an equal vote with men.

"AT THE FAIR" HALL DRIVING PARK OCT 3-4 1906. NEWMARKET, N.H.

Depicted above is the Grange Fair that took place October 3 and 4, 1906, at the Hall Driving Park (now the Trotter Park Subdivision off Parker's Falls Road), which used to exist as a horse racing track in Newmarket. Below, spectators are lined up to observe what could be a race, which was a big part of the culture back then.

"AT THE FAIR" HALL DRIVING PARK OCT 3-4-1906 NEWMARKET, N.H.

HORSE RACES

Hall's Driving Park
Newmarket, N. H.

MONDAY, MAY 30
1939

Program 10c

The cover of this pamphlet pretty much says it all. Horse racing thrived in Newmarket. Hall's Driving Park was a recreational hot spot and drew in crowds locally and from abroad.

The photograph above shows a local resident in a racing cart called a sulky, which is harnessed to the animal. Racers may have been able to get custom harnesses like this at H.G. Reilly's Perkins Express Harness shop in town. The photograph below is a touch blurry but is the clearest representation of local harness racing. Both men in their sulkies are guiding their horses to the finish line. The grandstand would have been lining the other side of the track, presumably where the photographer is seated.

At Pine Grove Park July 4th 1910.
Newmarket wins from Somersworth
Newmarket, N.H.
Photo by Thibault.
#64

Baseball is a timeless tradition that is a favorite in almost any town in America. Newmarket, in that respect, was no different—though citizens did seem to piece together a wide array of different teams for competitive play. Pine Grove Park was the site of this game after the great parade mentioned earlier. Many games were played in the park, and crowds were always plentiful. Note the boys sitting atop the grandstand. Below, the Old Timers, a traveling team that competed regionally, was formed by players from teams from surrounding towns. They are older area all-stars who still had the competitive fire in their hearts.

"The Old Timers"
Photo by Thibault. 9/12/08.

Newmarket Manufacturing Company also pieced together a team of players that competed against other teams from businesses around the area as well as with the town's own team. Just because an athlete had graduated from the high school did not mean his playing days were over. Baseball was a recreational activity that people played all the time—before television and other forms of technology became the predominant entertainment forms.

The Lafayette Club was a fraternal social and athletic organization that was geared toward French Canadians affiliated with Catholicism. The club was an active social society during the late 1800s; however, it seems to have disappeared after World War II. The club pieced together baseball teams of its own, including the team showcased in this photograph from 1901. A closer look shows that these men are wearing roller skates, thus making them early adopters of roller hockey. The above image has the entire club posing outside of their meetinghouse. Members of the club were also known as champion card players.

The Newmarket Gun Club was a collective of townsmen who enjoyed the hunt and the camaraderie that went along with it. It is rumored that it was perhaps shut down due to fundraising tactics. Notice the string of various slain fowl. A fashion trend at this time (early 1900s) was decorative feather hats worn by both men and women. The gun club was accused of hunting down too many birds used solely for the sale of feathers for said hats.

Camp Montagnard was a summer retreat set up by Rev. Sullivan Kimball of the Baptist church. The camp was established on his property on Dame Road in the early 1900s, which contained various cabins. Reverend Kimball brought in international and local kids to enjoy sports, other summertime activities, and the company of their peers.

This is an image of foresters enjoying a social picnic. The man telling stories and keeping the clan entertained in the middle is noted as a Mr. Levasseaur. First established nationally in 1883, the Catholic Order of Foresters is a not-for-profit fraternal insurance organization that has over 137,000 members today.

Park Hill on Elm Street was the scene for this gathering in 1909. A note on the back of the picture claims that this is an outing following an Eagles baseball game. The Lamprey Aerie 1934 was officially instituted on May 19, 1910, in the Newmarket Town Hall by the District Grand Worthy Justice John Webb of Portsmouth, assisted by Aeries of Somersworth, Portsmouth, Dover, and Haverhill, Massachusetts. The group is still in existence, as is Park Hill, which still plays host to myriad baseball-related traffic today.

Local firemen are noted for lively social gatherings. These events were usually accented with the tradition of a summertime New England–style lobster/clambake. Also included in the festivities were cigars and kegs. All of the above (and even a lone white horse) can be seen within the compositions of the two photographs on this page. Camaraderie was the springboard to a cohesive working unit. The sentiment of "work hard, play hard" is on display at these firemen socials.

The above image is a group shot of the Harvest Club, which is an offshoot of the Grange, shown below, whose members were responsible for the Grange Fair events pictured earlier. The Grange also provided dramatic, musical, and educational presentations and social events that were open to entire community. The Grange was very active in the Newmarket community throughout the Great Depression and World War II. During the war, Newmarket high school students were actively involved in community projects as a direct result of influence from the Grange. After the war, Grange membership dwindled as townspeople became more engaged in industry rather than agriculture. The State University Co-operative Exchanges and 4-H groups later picked up farming interests.

The Improved Order of Red Men, Pocasset Tribe No. 45, was a patriotic fraternity chartered by Congress. Newmarket's chapter, known as the Red Man Club, organized to support charitable organizations and create lasting friendships with the community. Given the rich Native American history that is associated with Newmarket and the peaceful Squamscott tribe that existed in the area prior to the English settlers' arrival, it made perfect sense to have a social group that celebrated their culture. This photograph was taken in the hall of the top floor of the former Creighton Block, which is the site of the American Legion today.

Theater was a big piece of Newmarket culture from the late 1800s and early 1900s on through to the present day. The Lamprey Players were a social troupe that gathered to produce and promote theatrical productions around town. Theater was one of the primary forms of entertainment, with productions taking place at locations such as the town hall and upon the stage located on the second story of the Stone Church.

The first meeting of the Robert G. Durgin American Legion Post 67 of Newmarket was held on December 14, 1919, at the Red Men's Hall and was presided over by the temporary chairman, Mathes B. Griffin, who was elected the first commander of the post on January 16, 1920. The post was named for Robert G. Durgin of Newmarket, who was lost at sea en route to France with the 73rd Coast Artillery. The Gold Star, which his mother received, has a place of honor at the historical society. Many of the first meetings were held both at the Red Men's Hall and the Eagles Aerie until January 10, 1924, when the members engaged a room over the Newmarket National Bank. In these photographs, American Legion members are engaging with town youth as they make a charitable drop.

The Pool Hall was located in what was known as the Creighton Block, which can be seen directly across the street from the photographs focusing on the American Legion. The irony at play here is the fact that the legion is now in that very spot (after Creighton Block burned, they built their new facility there). The poolroom was a local hangout owned by Jean Baptiste LaPorte, who stands on the left with the pool stick in his hand.

The first Masonic lodge in Newmarket was formed in 1826 by 25 men, with Benjamin Wheatland chosen as worshipful master. The members held meetings in a factory store rented to them by the Newmarket Manufacturing Company (above the present-day location of Panzanella's Pizzeria on Main Street). The current lodge is directly above Crackskull's Books and Café.

The Fraternal Order of Eagles Aerie 1934 (Newmarket Eagle Drum Corps) is pictured here after marching in the Americanization Day parade in Dover on May 18, 1941. Though the drum corps is not longer in existence, the group is still active today and very much a supporter of local charities and communal fellowship. The drum corps marched in many local parades in honor of men and women who served in the armed forces.

The Newmarket Cornet Band was a longtime institution that was very active in local parades and other social gatherings where band music was applicable. The band was a collective of local musicians who enjoyed marching and making music together. A close look at the image shows who might be spying on the band from behind the trees in the background.

This is a classic c. 1910 photograph of the Newmarket Cornet Band gracing the stairs of the town library. The ornate uniforms really pop in this sharp composition. There was not any real underlying agenda for the band. For members, it was just about the march, the song, and being community participants. They embodied the true spirit of town residents, including mutual friendships. The Newmarket Cornet Band served the community one note at a time.

"MEMORIAL DAY" 1910.
NEWMARKET, N.H.
PHOTO BY THIBAULT.

Memorial Day is an important holiday in the town of Newmarket. Many have served in town, and there are monuments celebrating them. Parades back in the early 1900s were huge events, and people made it a point to see and be seen in those times. Community was very important. In this parade, which took place in 1910, the Newmarket Cornet Band marches in appreciation of those that have taken up arms, including the group of men in the image below, who are surviving members of the Civil War. These men are, from left to right, (first row) Alanson Haines, Cyrus Rand, and David A. Stevens; (second row) Franklin Brackett and George Murch.

These two photographs focus on the existence of the Newmarket Militia, which was formed to march during the celebration of Newmarket's 250th anniversary, which took place over the span of 10 days in late August 1977. At the outset, the militia was formed under the guidance of well-known Newmarket residents L. Forbes Getchell and Maj. Richard Shanda. This image shows the parade up Main Street, which occurred near the end of the anniversary celebration.

The winner of the festivity's best beard competition was the late John Jakubowicz, who was the eldest member of the militia and color guard (he is marching with the flag in the image above). It is worth nothing that in his youth, Jakubowicz happened to be one of the weavers at the Newmarket Manufacturing Company.

After years of planning and work, Newmarket's downtown is in full swing. Developed by Chinburg Properties, the revitalization of the mills into residential and retail properties has—without doubt—breathed new life into the town and given new life to the old granite blocks of the renowned industrial mills. Newmarket is a desired destination for visitors as well as those looking to take residence in Seacoast, New Hampshire. With the redevelopment, the mills are once again a working entity, like the one established as the economic backbone of Newmarket at the mills' inception in the town's earliest days. Historic preservation of these riverside structures celebrates the working tradition of the past while working to build and maintain Newmarket as the vibrant, thriving community that it is today.

Visit us at
arcadiapublishing.com